CW00486886

THE COMPREHENSIVE PALEO DIET COOKBOOK

THE COMPLETE COOKBOOK TO GET YOU STARTED: LOSE WEIGHT, BOOST YOUR METABOLISM, AND STAY HEALTHY WITH RECIPES THAT PRACTICALLY COOK THEMSELVES

JAYLEE BECK

TABLE OF CONTENTS:

CHAPTER 1: BREAKFAST

SWEET POTATO CASSEROLE WITH COCONUT

Prep:
30 mins
Cook:
40 mins
Total:
1 hr 10 mins
Servings:
8
Yield:
8 servings

INGREDIENTS:
3 large sweet potatoes
3 tablespoons butter, softened
1 cup packed brown sugar
1 cup chopped pecans
1 cup flaked coconut (Optional)
⅓ cup all-purpose flour
½ cup white sugar
2 eggs
¼ cup milk
1 tablespoon grated orange zest
3 tablespoons butter
1 teaspoon vanilla extract
½ teaspoon salt

DIRECTIONS:

1

Preheat oven to 350 degrees F (175 degrees C). Poke holes in the sweet potatoes with a fork, arrange the sweet potatoes on a cookie sheet. Grease an 11x7 inch glass baking dish.

2

Bake sweet potatoes for 1 hour. Let cool, then mash in a large bowl. There should be approximately 3 2/3 cups of mashed sweet potato.

3

Combine softened butter with brown sugar, nuts, coconut and flour; stir with a fork. Set aside.

4

Combine sugar, eggs, milk, orange peel, butter, vanilla, salt with the mashed sweet potatoes. Beat the mixture with an electric mixer until smooth. Pour mixture into prepared baking dish. Sprinkle the brown sugar-nut mixture over the top of the mixture.

5

Bake for 35 minutes.

NUTRITION FACTS:

444 calories; protein 4.8g; carbohydrates 57.4g; fat 23.3g; cholesterol 70mg

CRAWFORD BERRY SMOOTHIE

Prep:
10 mins
Total:
10 mins
Servings:
1
Yield:
1 smoothie

INGREDIENTS:
1 cup whole strawberries
1 cup soy milk
1 banana
1 tablespoon agave nectar
1 tablespoon ground flax seed meal
¼ teaspoon vanilla extract

DIRECTIONS:
1
Blend strawberries, soy milk, banana, agave nectar, flax seed, and vanilla extract in a blender until creamy.

NUTRITION FACTS:
386 calories; protein 11.5g; carbohydrates 72.2g; fat 8.1g;

SWEET POTATO HASH BROWN

Prep:
15 mins
Cook:
30 mins
Total:
45 mins
Servings:
4
Yield:
4 servings

INGREDIENTS:
2 tablespoons olive oil
½ cup diced sweet onion
3 sweet potatoes, peeled and grated
¼ pound cooked and diced lean bacon
1 ½ tablespoons minced fresh chives
1 ½ tablespoons chopped fresh parsley
¾ teaspoon chopped fresh thyme
salt and ground black pepper to taste

DIRECTIONS:

1

Heat olive oil in a large skillet over medium heat; cook and stir onion until lightly browned, 10 to 12 minutes. Add grated sweet potatoes; cook and stir until tender, about 15 minutes.

2

Increase heat to high and cook sweet potato mixture without stirring for 2 minutes. Reduce heat to medium and stir in bacon, chives, parsley, thyme, salt, and pepper.

NUTRITION FACTS:

405 calories; protein 14.2g; carbohydrates 45.3g; fat 18.8g;

EGG IN A HOLE

Prep:
1 min
Cook:
4 mins
Total:
5 mins
Servings:
1
Yield:
1 serving

INGREDIENTS:
1 ½ teaspoons bacon grease
1 slice bread
1 egg
salt and ground black pepper to taste

DIRECTIONS:

1

Melt the bacon grease in a non-stick pan over low heat.

2

Cut a 1 1/2 to 2-inch hole from the center of the bread slice; lay in the hot skillet. When the side facing down is lightly toasted, about 2 minutes, flip and crack the egg into the hole; season with salt and pepper. Continue to cook until the egg is cooked and mostly firm. Flip again and cook 1 minute more to assure doneness on both sides. Serve immediately.

NUTRITION FACTS:

231 calories; protein 8.7g; carbohydrates 13.1g; fat 15.9g

BROCCOLI TOTS

Prep:
30 mins
Cook:
34 mins
Additional:
10 mins
Total:
1 hr 14 mins
Servings:
4
Yield:
4 servings

INGREDIENTS:
1 (12 ounce) bag broccoli florets
2 teaspoons sea salt, divided
¾ cup finely shredded Cheddar cheese
½ cup panko bread crumbs
⅓ cup minced onion
1 large egg
2 tablespoons chopped fresh parsley
2 cloves garlic, grated
1 teaspoon ground cumin
½ teaspoon ground black pepper
2 tablespoons olive oil, or to taste

DIRECTIONS:

1

Preheat oven to 400 degrees F (200 degrees C). Line a baking sheet with parchment paper.

2

Place 1/2 of the broccoli florets in a food processor; pulse about 20 times until it looks like grains of rice. Repeat with remaining broccoli florets.

3

Fill a large, shallow saucepan with 1/2 inch water; add 1 teaspoon salt. Bring to a boil. Reduce heat to low and add broccoli rice. Cover and simmer until tender, about 5 minutes. Drain and let cool, about 10 minutes.

4

Transfer broccoli rice to the center of a clean absorbent dish towel. Squeeze and twist the towel to remove as much of the moisture as possible.

5

Mix Cheddar cheese, bread crumbs, onion, egg, parsley, garlic, cumin, and black pepper together in a large bowl. Mix in broccoli rice until mixture sticks together when pressed into a ball.

6

Scoop 1 1/2 tablespoons of mixture with a small ice cream scoop; form into a ball and press into the shape of a tot using oiled hands. Place on the prepared baking sheet. Repeat with remaining mixture.

7

Drizzle olive oil over broccoli tots. Sprinkle remaining 1 teaspoon salt on top.

8

Bake in the preheated oven, turning halfway with tongs, until golden brown, about 24 minutes.

NUTRITION FACTS:
256 calories; protein 12.2g; carbohydrates 17.7g; fat 17.5g;

BROCCOLI CHEDDAR FRITTATA

Prep:
15 mins
Cook:
15 mins
Additional:
10 mins
Total:
40 mins
Servings:
8
Yield:
8 servings

INGREDIENTS:
7 large eggs
¼ cup heavy cream
1 teaspoon smoked paprika
salt and freshly ground black pepper to taste
2 tablespoons unsalted butter
½ cup chopped onion
1 ½ cups chopped fresh broccoli
1 cup frozen diced hash brown potatoes, thawed
1 cup shredded Cheddar cheese
4 slices bacon, cooked and crumbled

DIRECTIONS:

1

Position a rack in the center of the oven and preheat the oven to 400 degrees F (200 degrees C).

2

Whisk eggs, cream, smoked paprika, salt, and pepper together in a bowl. Set aside.

3

Melt butter in a 12-inch nonstick, oven-proof skillet over medium-high heat until bubbly. Add chopped onion and cook until softened, 1 to 2 minutes. Add chopped broccoli and cook, stirring occasionally, about 2 minutes. Add potatoes and cook, stirring occasionally, about 2 minutes. Lightly season vegetables with additional salt and pepper.

4

Gently pat the vegetables into an even layer with the back of a spatula or spoon and turn off the heat. Sprinkle cheese over the vegetables, followed by bacon.

5

Pour the egg mixture into the skillet and gently shake to eliminate any holes around the vegetables. Let the residual heat cook the eggs slightly, about 2 minutes.

6

Bake in the preheated oven for 8 to 10 minutes. Check for doneness by using a knife to cut the center slightly. Eggs should not be runny enough to fill the cut. Allow to cool in the skillet for 5 minutes before serving.

NUTRITION FACTS:

179 calories; protein 7.7g; carbohydrates 6.2g; fat 15.2g;

PLANTAIN EGG ROLLS

Prep:
20 mins
Cook:
4 mins
Total:
24 mins
Servings:
20
Yield:
20 servings

INGREDIENTS:
1 cup white sugar
¼ cup water
20 spring roll wrappers
5 plantains, peeled and quartered
⅓ cup brown sugar
1 ½ cups vegetable oil

DIRECTIONS:

1

Put sugar and water in separate bowls. Separate spring roll wrappers; stack. Peel plantains; cut in half and then half again lengthwise.

2

Place 1 wrapper on a clean work surface with 1 corner facing you. Coat 1 plantain piece in sugar; place 1 inch from the near corner of the wrapper. Fold corner over the plantain; roll up halfway. Fold in 2 side corners; continue rolling until near the top. Moisten top corner with wet fingers; finish rolling. Repeat with remaining wrappers.

3

Heat oil in a deep-fryer or large saucepan to 350 degrees F (175 degrees C). Place egg rolls in a single layer; fry until golden brown on the bottom, 2 to 3 minutes. Flip; sprinkle with brown sugar. Fry 2 to 3 minutes more. Transfer egg rolls to a plate.

NUTRITION FACTS:

145 calories; protein 1.4g; carbohydrates 32.5g; fat 1.9g;

PALEO BREAD

Prep:
15 mins
Cook:
15 mins
Additional:
5 mins
Total:
35 mins
Servings:
6
Yield:
6 servings

INGREDIENTS:
2 large plantains, peeled and broken into chunks
2 eggs
1 tablespoon olive oil, or more to taste
salt to taste

DIRECTIONS:

1

Preheat oven to 350 degrees F (175 degrees C). Line a baking sheet with a silicone baking mat or parchment paper.

2

Blend plantain, eggs, olive oil, and salt in a food processor until smooth, scraping down sides occasionally. Spread plantain mixture into a rectangle about 1/2-inch thick onto the prepared baking sheet; sprinkle salt over the top.

3

Bake in the preheated oven until bread is lightly browned and holds together, about 15 minutes. Cool on pan for about 5 minutes before slicing with a pizza cutter.

NUTRITION FACTS:

156 calories; protein 3.3g; carbohydrates 29.4g; fat 4.2g; cholesterol 62mg;

CHAPTER 2: LUNCH

PUMPKIN BEAN SOUP

Prep:
15 mins
Cook:
35 mins
Total:
50 mins
Servings:
4
Yield:
6 cups

INGREDIENTS:
1 tablespoon olive oil
1 red bell pepper, chopped
1 onion, chopped
2 cloves garlic, minced
1 teaspoon ground cumin
1 (15 ounce) can pumpkin puree
1 (15 ounce) can black beans, rinsed and drained
1 (14 ounce) can whole kernel corn, drained
2 cups chicken broth
1 (8 ounce) can tomato sauce

1 teaspoon fresh cilantro leaves, finely chopped (Optional)
salt and pepper to taste
½ cup heavy cream, whipped (Optional)
¼ cup fresh chopped cilantro, for garnish (Optional)

DIRECTIONS:

1

Heat the olive oil in a saucepan over medium heat. Stir in the bell pepper and onion; cook and stir until the onion has softened and turned translucent, about 5 minutes. Mix in the garlic and cumin and cook, stirring, for an additional 2 minutes.

2

Pour in the pumpkin puree, black beans, corn, chicken broth, tomato sauce, and 1 teaspoon cilantro; season to taste with salt and pepper. Bring the soup to a gentle boil; reduce the heat and simmer, covered, for 25 minutes.

3

Garnish each bowl of soup with a dollop of unsweetened whipped cream and additional cilantro, if desired.

NUTRITION FACTS:

248 calories; protein 6g; carbohydrates 38.7g; fat 10.5g;

SOUTHERN BROCCOLI AND CAULIFLOWER SALAD

Prep:
25 mins
Cook:
10 mins
Additional:
30 mins
Total:
1 hr 5 mins
Servings:
12
Yield:
12 servings

INGREDIENTS:
1 (12 ounce) package bacon
6 cups broccoli florets
6 cups cauliflower florets
2 cups slivered almonds
1 ½ cups golden raisins
1 cup grated sharp Cheddar cheese
1 medium red onion, finely chopped
2 stalks celery, finely chopped

Dressing:
1 cup mayonnaise
1 cup sour cream
1 (8 ounce) package cream cheese, softened
½ cup white sugar
¼ cup lemon juice

DIRECTIONS:

1

Place bacon in a large skillet and cook over medium-high heat, turning occasionally, until evenly browned, about 10 minutes. Drain bacon slices on paper towels until cool enough to handle, then chop into small pieces.

2

Place bacon in a very large bowl with broccoli, cauliflower, almonds, raisins, Cheddar cheese, red onion, and celery.

3

Whisk together mayonnaise, sour cream, cream cheese, sugar, and lemon juice in a separate bowl until creamy. Pour over broccoli-cauliflower mixture; stir until well combined. Refrigerate until flavors have melded, at least 30 minutes

NUTRITION FACTS:
643 calories; protein 14.7g; carbohydrates 37.5g; fat 50.5g;

CREAM OF ASPARAGUS AND MUSHROOM SOUP

Prep:
15 mins
Cook:
40 mins
Total:
55 mins
Servings:
8
Yield:
8 servings

INGREDIENTS:
3 slices bacon
1 tablespoon bacon drippings
¼ cup butter
3 stalks celery, chopped
1 onion, diced
3 tablespoons all-purpose flour
6 cups chicken broth
1 potato, peeled and diced
1 pound fresh asparagus, tips set aside and stalks chopped
salt and ground black pepper to taste
1 (8 ounce) package sliced fresh mushrooms
¾ cup half-and-half cream

DIRECTIONS:

1

Place the bacon in a large, deep skillet, and cook over medium-high heat, turning occasionally, until evenly browned, about 10 minutes. Drain the bacon slices on a paper towel-lined plate. Crumble bacon when cool; set aside. Reserve 1 tablespoon of bacon drippings.

2

Melt butter with drippings in a saucepan over medium heat.

3

Cook and stir celery and onion in the saucepan until onion is translucent, about 4 minutes.

4

Whisk flour into the mixture and cook for 1 minute.

5

Whisk in chicken broth and bring to a boil.

6

Add potato and chopped asparagus stalks, reserving the asparagus tips for later. Season with salt and ground black pepper.

7

Reduce heat and simmer for 20 minutes.

8

Pour the soup into a blender, filling the pitcher no more than halfway full. Hold down the lid of the blender with a folded kitchen towel, and carefully start the blender, using a few quick pulses to get the soup moving before leaving it on to puree. Puree in batches until smooth and pour into a clean pot. Alternately, you can use a stick blender and puree the soup right in the cooking pot.

9

Cook and stir mushrooms and asparagus tips in the same skillet used for bacon until mushrooms give up their liquid, 5 to 8 minutes. Season with salt and ground black pepper, if needed.

10

Stir mushrooms, asparagus tips, and half-and-half cream to pureed soup. Cook until thoroughly heated.

11

Garnish soup with crumbled bacon.

NUTRITION FACTS:
155 calories; protein 5.2g; carbohydrates 12.7g; fat 10g;

MIXED SEAFOOD OKRA

Prep:
20 mins
Cook:
15 mins
Total:
35 mins
Servings:
6
Yield:
6 servings

INGREDIENTS:
2 tablespoons vegetable oil
1 medium onion, halved and sliced
1 tablespoon minced fresh ginger root
1 tablespoon minced garlic
1 (14 ounce) can light coconut milk
3 tablespoons lime juice
1 tablespoon curry paste, or more to taste
1 tablespoon brown sugar
12 medium shrimp, peeled (tails left on) and deveined
12 sea scallops, halved
6 ounces asparagus, cut into 2-inch pieces
2 tablespoons chopped cilantro
salt to taste

DIRECTIONS:

1

Heat oil in a large skillet over medium-high heat. Saute onion, ginger, and garlic in hot oil until onion starts to soften, 2 to 3 minutes. Stir coconut milk, lime juice, curry paste, and brown sugar into onion mixture, bring to a simmer and cook until slightly reduced, about 5 minutes.

2

Stir shrimp, scallops, asparagus, cilantro, and salt into onion mixture; cook until shrimp and scallops are no longer transparent in the center, about 5 minutes

NUTRITION FACTS:

166 calories; protein 8.9g; carbohydrates 7.8g; fat 10.9g;

LEMON TROUT

Prep:
10 mins
Cook:
20 mins
Total:
30 mins
Servings:
4
Yield:
4 servings

INGREDIENTS:
4 cups all-purpose flour
2 tablespoons lemon pepper
1 ½ tablespoons salt
½ teaspoon dried thyme
½ teaspoon cayenne pepper
1 teaspoon onion powder
¼ cup grated lemon zest, divided
4 (6 ounce) fillets rainbow trout
1 lemon
½ cup lemon juice
½ cup extra-virgin olive oil

DIRECTIONS:

1

In a large bowl, stir together the flour, lemon pepper, salt, thyme, cayenne and half of the lemon zest. Combine the lemon juice and remaining lemon zest in a shallow dish and soak fish fillets for about 1 minute.

2

Heat oil in a large skillet over medium heat. Dip the trout fillets in the flour mixture so that both sides are coated. Shake off the excess and place fillets in the hot oil. Cook for 3 to 4 minutes on each side, until golden brown and fish can be flaked with a fork. Discard the leftover lemon juice.

3

Remove from the skillet and drain on paper towels briefly before serving. Garnish each serving with a wedge of lemon.

NUTRITION FACTS:

979 calories; protein 48.6g; carbohydrates 103.1g; fat 40.5g;

BEEF AND NOODLES

Prep:
20 mins
Cook:
1 hr 10 mins
Total:
1 hr 30 mins
Servings:
4
Yield:
4 servings

INGREDIENTS:
1 pound sirloin steak, cut into 1-inch cubes
2 tablespoons butter
1 large onion, sliced
1 cup beef stock
2 bay leaves
1 pinch dried thyme
salt and ground black pepper to taste
1 cup frozen peas
1 tablespoon cornstarch
4 cups egg noodles

DIRECTIONS:

1

Heat a skillet over medium-high heat; cook steak, working in batches, until seared and browned on all sides, about 5 minutes. Transfer seared steak to a plate.

2
Melt butter in the same skillet over medium heat and saute onion until softened, 5 to 10 minutes. Add steak to onion and pour beef stock over steak; season with bay leaves, thyme, salt, and pepper. Bring to a boil, reduce heat to low, cover skillet with a lid, and simmer until steak is tender, 50 minutes to 1 hour 50 minutes. Stir peas and cornstarch into steak mixture; cook uncovered until liquid thickens, about 10 minutes.

3
Bring a large pot of lightly salted water to a boil. Cook egg noodles in the boiling water, stirring occasionally until cooked through but firm to the bite, about 5 minutes; drain. Serve beef mixture over noodles.

NUTRITION FACTS:
402 calories; protein 28.5g; carbohydrates 38.7g; fat 14.4g;

SUMMER VEGGIE SALAD

Prep:
20 mins
Cook:
5 mins
Additional:
1 hr
Total:
1 hr 25 mins
Servings:
8
Yield:
8 servings

INGREDIENTS:
5 ears corn, husked
1 (15 ounce) can black beans, rinsed and drained
2 avocados, diced
1 bunch fresh cilantro, roughly chopped
1 pint cherry tomatoes, halved
¼ large red onion, thinly sliced
1 jalapeno pepper, seeded and chopped
¼ cup olive oil
2 limes, zested and juiced

DIRECTIONS:

1

Place corn into a large pot and cover with water; bring to a boil. Reduce heat to medium-low and simmer until tender, about 5 minutes. Drain and cool corn. Cut kernels from cob.

2

Mix corn kernels, black beans, avocados, cilantro, tomatoes, onion, and jalapeno pepper together in a bowl.

3

Whisk olive oil, lime zest, and lime juice together in a bowl; pour over corn mixture and toss to coat. Refrigerate until chilled, about 1 hour

NUTRITION FACTS:
282 calories; protein 7.7g; carbohydrates 34.4g; fat 15.5g;

CHAPTER 3: DINNER

BROCCOLI BITES

Prep:
10 mins
Cook:
10 mins
Total:
20 mins
Servings:
12
Yield:
2 dozen

INGREDIENTS:
3 tablespoons prepared Dijon-style mustard
4 tablespoons honey
2 cups broccoli florets
1 cup shredded Cheddar cheese
1 egg
1 cup milk
½ cup sifted all-purpose flour
½ teaspoon baking powder
½ teaspoon salt
½ teaspoon vegetable oil
½ cup vegetable oil for frying

DIRECTIONS:

1

To make the sauce: In a small bowl, stir together the mustard and honey. Set aside.

2

Chop florets into small pieces or pulse lightly in food processor. Toss in a mixing bowl with shredded cheese. Set aside.

3

Beat egg and stir in the milk. Sift flour, baking powder, and salt together and combine them with the egg and milk mixture, beating well. Beat in 1/2 teaspoon oil as well. Pour mixture over broccoli and cheese and toss to coat well.

4

In a large skillet or saucepan heat oil to 375 degrees F (190 degrees C).

5

Drop broccoli mixture by spoonfuls into 375 degrees F (190 degrees C) oil and fry until golden brown. Serve with honey mustard sauce.

NUTRITION FACTS:

113 calories; protein 4.5g; carbohydrates 12.6g; fat 5.1g;

RICOTTA STUFFED SQUASH

Servings:
8
Yield:
8 servings

INGREDIENTS:
8 yellow squash
2 tablespoons butter
1 onion, chopped
1 clove garlic, minced
1 (10 ounce) package frozen chopped spinach, thawed
2 eggs
2 cups ricotta cheese
¼ cup grated Parmesan cheese
1 tablespoon chopped fresh parsley
½ teaspoon salt
1 teaspoon Italian seasoning
1 pinch ground black pepper
1 (26 ounce) jar spaghetti sauce

DIRECTIONS:

1

Preheat oven to 375 degrees F (190 degrees C).

2

Trim off ends of squash; cut squash in half (lengthwise). With a teaspoon scoop out seeds and part of the pulp leaving shells about 1/2 inch thick. Steam squash shells over boiling water until crisp-tender (about 5 minutes). Plunge into cold water, drain well and set aside.

3

In a small frying pan over medium heat, melt one tablespoon of the butter. Add onion and garlic and cook until they are done. Squeeze the spinach to remove extra moisture and add to the garlic and onion and cook until thoroughly heated.

4

In a medium size mixing bowl, combine eggs, ricotta, Parmesan, parsley, salt, pepper, Italian seasoning and spinach mixture. Fill the squash halves with this mixture, about three tablespoons per shell and place squash in a shallow baking dish. Melt the remaining butter and brush over the squash shells

5

Bake for 20 minutes. If desired, serve with tomato sauce.

NUTRITION FACTS:
185 calories; protein 8.3g; carbohydrates 22.4g; fat 8.1g;

HAM AND BUTTERNUT SQUASH SPAGHETTI

Prep:
15 mins
Cook:
35 mins
Total:
50 mins
Servings:
4
Yield:
4 servings

INGREDIENTS:
2 tablespoons olive oil
4 ounces smoked ham, thinly sliced
3 cloves garlic, thinly sliced
1 ½ cups chicken broth
3 cups peeled, seeded, and diced butternut squash
1 pinch crushed red pepper flakes, or to taste
salt, or to taste
1 teaspoon ground black pepper, or to taste
1 cup mascarpone cheese
1 tablespoon chopped Italian flat leaf parsley
14 ounces spaghetti
finely grated Parmigiano-Reggiano cheese

DIRECTIONS:

1

Heat olive oil over medium heat in a large skillet. Stir in ham and cook until the edges are slightly browned, about 3 minutes.

2

Stir in garlic; cook until fragrant and edges are barely golden, about 1 minute.

3

Pour chicken broth over ham and garlic; bring to a simmer. Stir in butternut squash, red pepper flakes, and salt. Cook until squash is tender, about 15 minutes. Stir in black pepper and reduce heat to low.

4

Gently stir mascarpone cheese into squash mixture until completely incorporated. Stir in Italian parsley. Remove from heat and cover.

5

Bring a large pot of lightly salted water to a boil. Cook spaghetti in the boiling water, stirring occasionally until cooked through but firm to the bite, about 12 minutes. Drain and return to pot.

6

Pour butternut-mascarpone sauce over spaghetti, stirring until combined. Sprinkle Parmigiano-Reggiano cheese over spaghetti and serve.

NUTRITION FACTS:
808 calories; protein 25.3g; carbohydrates 87g; fat 41.1g

FRESH CORN AND ZUCCHINI SAUTE

Prep:
10 mins
Cook:
15 mins
Total:
25 mins
Servings:
4
Yield:
4 servings

INGREDIENTS:
¼ cup butter
½ small white onion, finely diced
3 small zucchinis, diced
3 ears corn, husks and silk removed
sea salt to taste
freshly ground black pepper to taste

DIRECTIONS:

1

Heat butter in a skillet over medium heat, stirring occasionally, until lightly browned, 1 to 2 minutes. Cook and stir onion in the melted butter until translucent, about 5 minutes. Cut kernels from the ears of corn. Add zucchini and corn; cook and stir until zucchini is tender, about 8 minutes. Season with sea salt and pepper.

NUTRITION FACTS:

178 calories; protein 3.5g; carbohydrates 16.8g; fat 12.5g;

PURPLE CABBAGE SALAD

Prep:
15 mins
Cook:
5 mins
Total:
20 mins
Servings:
4
Yield:
4 servings

INGREDIENTS:
2 ½ cups shredded red cabbage
1 (10 ounce) can mandarin oranges, drained
1 green onion, chopped
¼ cup sweetened dried cranberries
¼ cup pine nuts
⅓ cup canola oil
¼ cup vinegar
1 tablespoon white sugar
2 pinches salt

DIRECTIONS:
1
Lightly toss red cabbage, mandarin orange segments, green onion, and cranberries together in a salad bowl.

2

Toast pine nuts in a small skillet over medium heat, stirring constantly, until fragrant and lightly browned, about 2 minutes. Remove immediately to a bowl and let cool.

3

Whisk canola oil, vinegar, sugar, and salt in a bowl until sugar and salt have dissolved.

4

Stir toasted pine nuts into salad and pour dressing over the top. Toss again to coat salad with dressing.

NUTRITION FACTS:
291 calories; protein 3.2g; carbohydrates 20.9g; fat 23.1g;

GRILLED GREEN BEANS AND ONIONS

Prep:
10 mins
Cook:
15 mins
Total:
25 mins
Servings:
4
Yield:
4 servings

INGREDIENTS:
1 pound fresh green beans, trimmed
1 onion, chopped
1 tablespoon olive oil
1 teaspoon Diamond salt

DIRECTIONS:

1

Preheat outdoor grill to medium heat (400 degrees F.)

2

Toss the green beans and onions in a bowl with the olive oil and Diamond Crystal® Kosher Salt. Place mixture into a steamer basket or shallow grill pan.

3
Place on the grill and close the lid. Cook until beans and onions, stirring every 5 minutes, until veggies have a slight char, 10 to 15 minutes.

NUTRITION FACTS:
76 calories; protein 2.4g; carbohydrates 10.7g; fat 3.5g;

OLIVE OIL DIPPING SAUCE

Prep:
5 mins
Cook:
5 mins
Total:
10 mins
Servings:
16
Yield:
1 cup

INGREDIENTS:
1 cup extra-virgin olive oil
2 cloves garlic, minced
¼ teaspoon dried oregano
1 pinch salt, or to taste
1 pinch dried rosemary, or to taste
1 pinch dried basil, or to taste
ground black pepper to taste

DIRECTIONS:
1
Combine the olive oil, garlic, oregano, salt, rosemary, basil, and pepper in a skillet over medium heat; cook until the garlic begins to sizzle, about 5 minutes. Remove immediately from heat.

NUTRITION FACTS:
127 calories; protein 0.1g; carbohydrates 0.2g; fat 14g;

CHAPTER 4: SNACK & APPETIZERS

SALMON WRAPS

Prep:
10 mins
Total:
10 mins
Servings:
24
Yield:
24 servings

INGREDIENTS:
1 (8 ounce) package cream cheese, softened
2 tablespoons chopped fresh dill
2 tablespoons chopped fresh chives
1 tablespoon lemon juice
3 (8 inch) flour tortillas
6 slices smoked salmon

DIRECTIONS:

1

Mix cream cheese, dill, chives, and lemon juice together in a bowl.

2

Spread cream cheese on 1/3 of each tortilla. Lay 2 salmon slices on top; roll tightly and seal edges with a dab of cream cheese. Cut each roll into 1-inch segments.

NUTRITION FACTS:

61 calories; protein 2.5g; carbohydrates 3.7g; fat 4g; cholesterol 11.9mg;

HOMEMADE PALEO MAYO

rep:
5 mins
Total:
5 mins
Servings:
10
Yield:
10 servings

INGREDIENTS:
1 extra large egg
1 tablespoon lemon juice
1 teaspoon Dijon mustard
½ teaspoon sea salt, or to taste
1 pinch cayenne pepper, or to taste (Optional)
1 cup light olive oil

DIRECTIONS:
1
Combine egg, lemon juice, mustard, salt, and cayenne pepper in a blender; blend until smooth. Drizzle in olive oil, blending until the mixture thickens, about 5 minutes.

NUTRITION FACTS:
200 calories; protein 0.7g; carbohydrates 0.3g; fat 22.2g;

GARLIC, BASIL AND BACON DAVILED EGGS

Prep:
15 mins
Cook:
25 mins
Additional:
30 mins
Total:
1 hr 10 mins
Servings:
24
Yield:
24 stuffed egg halves

INGREDIENTS:
12 eggs
2 large cloves garlic, pressed
5 slices bacon
½ cup finely chopped fresh basil
⅓ cup mayonnaise
¼ teaspoon crushed red pepper flakes
salt and pepper to taste
¼ teaspoon paprika for garnish

DIRECTIONS:

1

Place the eggs into a saucepan in a single layer and fill with water to cover the eggs by 1 inch. Cover the saucepan and bring the water to a boil over high heat. Remove from the heat and let the eggs stand in the hot water for 15 minutes. Drain. Cool the eggs under cold running water. Peel once cold. Halve the eggs lengthwise and scoop the yolks into a bowl. Mash the yolks together with pressed garlic with a fork.

2

Cook the bacon in a large, deep skillet over medium-high heat until evenly browned, about 10 minutes. Drain on a paper towel-lined plate; chop once cool. Add to the mashed egg yolks. Stir the basil, mayonnaise, red pepper flakes, salt, and pepper into the mixture until evenly mixed. Fill the egg white halves with the mixture; sprinkle each stuffed egg with a bit of paprika.

NUTRITION FACTS:
69 calories; protein 3.9g; carbohydrates 0.5g; fat 5.7g;

PLANTAIN CHIPS

Prep:
15 mins
Cook:
20 mins
Total:
35 mins
Servings:
8
Yield:
8 servings

INGREDIENTS:
Vegetable oil, for deep-frying
2 green plantains, peeled and sliced 1/8-inch thick
salt to taste

DIRECTIONS:

1

Heat oil in deep-fryer to 375 degrees F (190 degrees C).

2

Deep fry the plantain slices, about a dozen at a time, until golden brown on both sides, 3 to 4 minutes. Drain in a large bowl lined with paper towels, and salt to taste while still warm.

NUTRITION FACTS:
103 calories; protein 0.6g; carbohydrates 14.3g; fat 5.7g;

SPINACH AND KALE SMOOTHIE

Prep:
10 mins
Total:
10 mins
Servings:
1
Yield:
1 serving

INGREDIENTS:
2 cups fresh spinach
1 cup almond milk
1 tablespoon peanut butter
1 tablespoon chia seeds (Optional)
1 leaf kale
1 sliced frozen banana

DIRECTIONS:

1

Blend spinach, almond milk, peanut butter, chia seeds, and kale together in a blender until smooth. Add banana and blend until smooth.

NUTRITION FACTS:
325 calories; protein 10g; carbohydrates 46.1g; fat 13.9g;

HONEY-PECAN MINI MUFFINS

Prep:
15 mins
Cook:
10 mins
Additional:
5 mins
Total:
30 mins
Servings:
24
Yield:
24 mini muffins

INGREDIENTS:
1 serving cooking spray
⅓ cup melted butter, at room temperature
¼ cup honey
2 large eggs, lightly beaten
1 teaspoon vanilla extract
½ cup light brown sugar
½ cup all-purpose flour
½ teaspoon baking powder
¼ teaspoon salt
1 cup chopped pecans

DIRECTIONS:

1

Preheat the oven to 425 degrees F (220 degrees C). Spray a 24-cup mini muffin tin with cooking spray.

2
Whisk butter, honey, eggs, and vanilla extract together in a bowl.

3
Stir brown sugar, flour, baking powder, and salt together in a bowl. Make a well in the center, and pour butter mixture into the well. Stir just until batter is combined.

4
Sprinkle 1/2 of the chopped pecans into the bottoms of the prepared muffin cups. Spoon batter evenly over top, until just about full and sprinkle with remaining pecans.

5
Bake in the preheated oven until a toothpick inserted in the center comes out clean, 10 to 12 minutes. Leave the muffins in the pan for about 5 minutes before removing to serve.

NUTRITION FACTS:
98 calories; protein 1.3g; carbohydrates 10.1g; fat 6.3g;

APRICOT ALMOND GALETTE

Prep:
20 mins
Cook:
40 mins
Total:
1 hr
Servings:
8
Yield:
1 8-inch galette

INGREDIENTS:
10 small fresh apricots, pitted and quartered
⅓ cup white sugar
1 cup almond meal
½ cup confectioners' sugar
1 egg
1 (9 inch) refrigerated pie crust
⅓ cup apricot jam, melted

DIRECTIONS:

1

Preheat an oven to 350 degrees F (175 degrees C). Roll out pie crust onto a baking sheet.

2

Toss the quartered apricots with the white sugar in a bowl. Mix almond meal, confectioners' sugar, and egg together in another bowl to create a paste. Spread almond paste on the center of the pie crust, leaving 1/2 inch of bare crust all around the edge. Arrange the sugared apricots over the almond paste. Fold the 1/2-inch bare edge of the crust inward over the almond paste and apricots, leaving the center of the tart uncovered. Crimp the edge down with a fork as you go around the tart.

3

Bake in the preheated oven until the crust is golden brown, about 40 minutes. Brush the melted apricot jam over the hot galette. Slice and serve.

NUTRITION FACTS:
290 calories; protein 8.3g; carbohydrates 42.6g; fat 10.8g;

BUTTER FRIED PARSNIPS

Prep:
10 mins
Cook:
20 mins
Total:
30 mins
Servings:
5
Yield:
4 to 6 servings

INGREDIENTS:
6 parsnips, peeled and quartered lengthwise
¼ cup all-purpose flour for coating
½ teaspoon seasoning salt
½ cup butter, melted

DIRECTIONS:
1
In a large saucepan cover parsnips with water, cover and boil over medium-high heat until tender, about 10 minutes. Drain.

2
In a plastic bag combine flour and seasoning salt. Dip parsnips in butter and place them in the bag. Shake bag to coat parsnips with the seasoned flour.

3
Heat the butter in a large skillet over medium-high heat. When the butter starts to sizzle, add parsnips. Cook, turning occasionally, until all sides are golden brown

NUTRITION FACTS:
305 calories; protein 3.1g; carbohydrates 33.5g; fat 19g;

CHAPTER 5: DESSERT

CHAFFLES AND ALMOND FLOUR

Prep:
5 mins
Cook:
10 mins
Additional:
5 mins
Total:
20 mins
Servings:
2
Yield:
2 4-inch chaffles

INGREDIENTS:
1 large egg
1 tablespoon blanched almond flour
¼ teaspoon baking powder
½ cup shredded mozzarella cheese
cooking spray

DIRECTIONS:

1

Whisk together egg, almond flour, and baking powder. Stir in mozzarella cheese and set batter aside.

2

Preheat a waffle iron according to manufacturer's instructions.

3

Spray both sides of the preheated waffle iron with cooking spray. Pour 1/2 of the batter onto the waffle iron and spread it out from the center with a spoon. Close the waffle maker and cook until chaffle reaches your desired doneness, about 3 minutes. Carefully lift chaffle out of the waffle iron and repeat with remaining batter. Allow chaffles to cool for 2 to 3 minutes, and they will begin to crisp up

NUTRITION FACTS:
132 calories; protein 10.8g; carbohydrates 2g; fat 9g

ORANGE-WALNUT MUFFINS

Prep:
15 mins
Cook:
15 mins
Additional:
10 mins
Total:
40 mins
Servings:
12
Yield:
12 muffins

INGREDIENTS:
1 cup all-purpose flour
1 ¼ cups whole wheat flour
¼ cup ground flaxseed
1 teaspoon baking soda
½ teaspoon salt
1 cup orange juice
2 egg whites
⅓ cup almond milk
3 tablespoons brown sugar
2 tablespoons honey
½ cup chopped walnuts

DIRECTIONS:

1

Preheat oven to 375 degrees F (190 degrees C). Grease 12 muffin cups or line with paper muffin liners.

2

Mix all-purpose flour, whole wheat flour, flaxseed, baking soda, and salt together in a small bowl.

3

Beat orange juice, egg whites, almond milk, brown sugar, and honey together in a large bowl until smooth. Stir flour mixture into the orange juice mixture just until the dry ingredients are moistened completely. Fold walnuts through the batter. Spoon batter into the prepared muffin cups.

4

Bake in preheated oven until lightly browned and a toothpick inserted into the center of a muffin comes out clean, 15 to 20 minutes. Cool in the pans for 10 minutes before removing to cool completely on a wire rack.

NUTRITION FACTS:

162 calories; protein 4.8g; carbohydrates 27g; fat 4.6g;

PEANUT BUTTER GRANOLA BARS

Prep:
10 mins
Cook:
5 mins
Additional:
15 mins
Total:
30 mins
Servings:
24
Yield:
24 bars

INGREDIENTS:
¼ cup peanut butter
⅓ (12 ounce) jar honey
¼ cup brown sugar
1 cup granola
1 cup quick cooking oats
1 cup puffed rice cereal
½ cup chocolate chips
½ cup chopped dried mixed fruit

DIRECTIONS:

1

Melt peanut butter and honey together in a saucepan over medium heat. Dissolve brown sugar into the peanut butter mixture; bring to a simmer for 2 minutes.

2

Mix granola, oats, rice cereal, chocolate chips, and fruit together in a large bowl; pour peanut butter mixture over the granola mixture and fold to coat.

3

Grease a cake pan. Pour the granola mixture into the prepared pan and press into a flat layer. Cool at room temperature until set, about 15 minutes before cutting into bars.

NUTRITION FACTS:
109 calories; protein 2.2g; carbohydrates 18g; fat 3.9g;

PEAR BUTTER

Prep:
30 mins
Cook:
1 min
Total:
31 mins
Servings:
32
Yield:
2 pints

INGREDIENTS:
4 pounds medium pears, quartered and cored
2 cups sugar
1 teaspoon grated orange zest
¼ teaspoon ground nutmeg
¼ cup orange juice

DIRECTIONS:
1
Place pears into a large pot over medium heat, and add just enough water to cover the bottom of the pot and keep them from sticking, about 1/2 cup. Cook until the pears are soft, about 30 minutes. Press pears through a sieve or food mill, and measure out 2 quarts of the pulp.

2

Pour the pear pulp and sugar into a large saucepan and stir to dissolve sugar. Stir in the orange zest, nutmeg and orange juice. Cook over medium heat until the mixture is thick enough to mound in a spoon. When the mixture begins to thicken, stir frequently to prevent scorching on the bottom. This will take about 1 hour.

3

Ladle the pear butter into hot sterile jars, leaving 1/4 inch of headspace. Remove air bubbles by sliding a metal spatula around where the pear butter touches the glass. Wipe jar rims clean, and seal with lids and rings. Process for 10 minutes in a boiling water bath. The water should cover the jars by 1 inch. Check with your local extension for exact processing times for your area.

NUTRITION FACTS:
82 calories; protein 0.2g; carbohydrates 21.5g; fat 0.1g;

CHIA COCONUT PUDDING WITH COCONUT MILK

Prep:
10 mins
Additional:
20 mins
Total:
30 mins
Servings:
6
Yield:
6 servings

INGREDIENTS:
½ cup chia seeds
2 cups coconut milk
6 tablespoons unsweetened coconut milk
1 tablespoon agave nectar, or more to taste
½ teaspoon vanilla extract
¼ teaspoon ground cinnamon
1 pinch salt
½ cup diced fresh strawberries (Optional)

DIRECTIONS:
1
Place chia seeds in a bowl.

2
Whisk coconut milk, unsweetened coconut milk, agave nectar, vanilla extract, cinnamon, and salt together in a bowl; pour over chia seeds and stir well. Allow coconut milk-chia seed mixture to soak until thickened, at least 20 minutes, or cover bowl with plastic wrap and refrigerate overnight.

3
Stir pudding and top with strawberries.

NUTRITION FACTS:
243 calories; protein 3.5g; carbohydrates 10.8g; fat 22.4g;

SWEET PLANTAIN PIE

Prep:
30 mins
Cook:
1 hr
Additional:
10 mins
Total:
1 hr 40 mins
Servings:
6
Yield:
6 servings

INGREDIENTS:
2 tablespoons canola oil
1 pound ground pork
2 ounces cooked ham, cut into small dice
½ cup sofrito
12 small pitted olives, chopped
1 tablespoon capers, drained and chopped
¾ teaspoon salt
¼ teaspoon garlic powder
¼ teaspoon dried oregano
½ cup tomato sauce
5 large plantains
¼ cup butter, softened
¾ teaspoon white sugar
2 tablespoons melted butter

DIRECTIONS:

1

Preheat an oven to 375 degrees F (190 degrees C). Butter a baking dish.

2

Heat the canola oil in a large skillet over medium-high heat. Cook the ground pork and cooked ham in the hot oil until the pork is completely cooked and no longer pink, 7 to 10 minutes. Remove from the skillet and set aside, reserving 2 tablespoons of the drippings in the skillet.

3

Reduce the heat to medium-low. Place the skillet over the heat and add the sofrito; cook and stir the sofrito for 5 minutes. Add the olives, capers, salt, garlic powder, oregano, and tomato sauce to the sofrito; cook and stir another 5 minutes. Return the ground pork and ham to the skillet and stir; simmer for 15 minutes, stirring a few times while it cooks.

4

Bring a pot of lightly salted water to a boil. Rinse the plantains and cut off their tips, leaving the skin on; cut each plantain into 2 to 3 segments each about 3 inches long. Cook the plantains in the boiling water until tender, about 15 minutes; drain and peel. Put the peeled plantains in a mixing bowl and mash with a potato masher. Add the softened butter and sugar; mix.

5

Spread about half of the plantain mixture into the bottom of the prepared baking dish. Layer the meat mixture over the plantains. Top with the remaining plantain mixture.

6

Bake in the preheated oven for 15 minutes. Brush the top with the melted butter and continue baking until the top is browned, about 10 minutes more. Remove from oven and allow to rest 10 to 15 minutes before slicing to serve.

NUTRITION FACTS:
643 calories; protein 19.9g; carbohydrates 76.1g; fat 32.5g;

DARK CHOCOLATE PUDDING

Prep:
5 mins
Cook:
15 mins
Additional:
8 hrs
Total:
8 hrs 20 mins
Servings:
4
Yield:
4 servings

INGREDIENTS:
1 cup white sugar, divided
2 tablespoons all-purpose flour
1 egg
2 cups milk
4 (1 ounce) squares semisweet dark chocolate
1 teaspoon vanilla extract

DIRECTIONS:

1

Mix 1/2 cup sugar and flour together in a small bowl.

2

Mix remaining sugar and egg in another bowl. Add to flour mixture and mix together.

3
Heat milk in a heavy saucepan over medium-low heat until warm, about 5 minutes; do not let boil. Stir sugar mixture into milk and cook over medium-high heat until it starts to bubble, about 5 minutes, stirring quickly the entire time to ensure it doesn't burn. Let bubble for at least 1 minute. Remove from heat and stir in chocolate and vanilla extract until smooth.

4
Pour pudding into serving bowls, cover, and refrigerate for 8 hours, to overnight.

NUTRITION FACTS:
440 calories; protein 7.6g; carbohydrates 75.7g; fat 12.9g;

HEALTHY PUMPKIN CRANBERRY MUFFIN

Prep:
25 mins
Cook:
25 mins
Additional:
5 mins
Total:
55 mins
Servings:
12
Yield:
1 dozen cupcakes

INGREDIENTS:
½ cup milk
1 ½ teaspoons white vinegar
½ cup whole wheat flour
½ cup all-purpose flour
½ cup quick cooking oats
1 teaspoon baking soda
¾ teaspoon ground ginger
½ teaspoon baking powder
½ teaspoon ground cinnamon
¼ teaspoon ground nutmeg
¼ teaspoon salt
1 cup canned pumpkin
½ cup packed brown sugar
¼ cup white sugar
2 tablespoons vegetable oil

1 egg
½ cup coarsely chopped fresh cranberries
¼ cup dried cranberries

DIRECTIONS:

1

Preheat oven to 375 degrees F (190 degrees C). Line 12 muffin cups with paper liners.

2

Stir milk and vinegar together in a small bowl.

3

Mix whole wheat flour, all-purpose flour, oats, baking soda, ginger, baking powder, cinnamon, nutmeg, and salt in a large bowl.

4

Whisk pumpkin, brown sugar, white sugar, vegetable oil, and egg together in a separate bowl; beat in milk mixture until smooth. Stir flour mixture into pumpkin mixture until just combined. Fold in fresh and dried cranberries. Spoon batter into the prepared muffin cups.

5

Bake in the preheated oven until a toothpick inserted in the center of a muffin comes out clean, about 25 minutes. Cool muffins in the pan for 5 minutes before removing to wire rack to cool completely.

NUTRITION FACTS:
149 calories; protein 2.8g; carbohydrates 28.1g; fat 3.4g;

EGG SOUFFLE

Prep:
15 mins
Cook:
45 mins
Additional:
13 hrs 20 mins
Total:
14 hrs 20 mins
Servings:
8
Yield:
7 to 10 servings

INGREDIENTS:
16 slices white bread, with crusts trimmed
8 ounces shredded Cheddar cheese
1 ½ cups shredded Swiss cheese, divided
7 eggs
3 cups milk
½ teaspoon onion powder
½ teaspoon Dijon mustard
3 cups cornflakes cereal
¼ cup margarine, melted

DIRECTIONS:

1

Lightly butter a 9x13 inch baking dish. Cut bread slices into 1/2 inch cubes. Line bottom of pan with one half of bread cubes. Sprinkle cheddar cheese and 1 cup Swiss cheese on top of bread cubes, reserve 1/2 cup Swiss cheese. Spread remaining bread cubes on top of cheese.

2

Mix the eggs, milk, onion powder and mustard. Pour egg mixture over the bread. Sprinkle the remaining 1/2 cup cheese over the egg mixture. Cover with foil and refrigerate overnight.

3

The next morning, preheat oven to 375 degrees F (190 degrees C). Place cornflakes in a bowl and drizzle with melted margarine. Spread cornflakes on top of casserole.

4

Bake in preheated oven for 30 minutes covered, then uncover and bake for an additional 15 minutes.

NUTRITION FACTS:

521 calories; protein 25.6g; carbohydrates 40.8g; fat 28.5g;

COCONUT LIME CUPCAKES

Prep:
25 mins
Cook:
20 mins
Total:
45 mins
Servings:
36
Yield:
36 cupcakes

INGREDIENTS:
2 cups white sugar
1 cup butter
4 eggs
1 tablespoon coconut extract
1 tablespoon vanilla extract
3 cups all-purpose flour
1 tablespoon baking powder
½ teaspoon baking powder
¼ teaspoon ground nutmeg
1 cup buttermilk
½ cup fresh lime juice
2 cups sweetened shredded coconut
2 tablespoons freshly grated lime zest

DIRECTIONS:

1

Preheat the oven to 350 degrees F (175 degrees C). Line 36 cupcake cups with paper liners.

2

Beat sugar and butter together in the bowl of an electric stand mixer until fluffy, about 10 minutes. Beat in eggs, 1 at a time, adding coconut extract and vanilla extract with the last egg.

3

Combine flour, 1 tablespoon plus 1/2 teaspoon baking powder, and nutmeg in another bowl. Beat into the egg mixture until thoroughly combined; beat in buttermilk and lime juice. Stir in coconut and lime zest.

4

Fill each of the prepared cupcake cups with about 1/4 cup of batter using a large cookie scoop.

5

Bake in the preheated oven until a toothpick inserted into the center of a cupcake comes out clean, 20 to 25 minutes. Remove from the oven and let cool before serving.

NUTRITION FACTS:

159 calories; protein 2.2g; carbohydrates 22.1g; fat 7g;